The Alm
John Wesley'
In Toda

www.hargreavespublishing.com

www.facebook.com/hargreavespublishing

www.twitter.com/hargreavesbooks

Contents

Translator's preface

John Wesley led one of the greatest Christian revivals in the history of England, and his open air preaching saw many thousands of conversions all across Great Britain. The 'Forty-Four Sermons' which he compiled for use by Methodist Local Preachers remains a timeless classic, and a definitive collection of core Wesleyan doctrine, along with his Notes on the New Testament.

Forty-Four Sermons was first published in 1759, over 250 years ago, and since then the English language has changed and evolved to the point that his works can no longer be easily read and understood in their original dialect. Therefore to preserve Wesley's message and to allow it to come to life for a new generation, this project has been undertaken.

Many of John and Charles Wesley's views can be seen as products of the day and age in which they lived. The passion they preached with, and the relentless conviction behind their words changed Britain, some say prevented a civil uprising and revolution, and in many ways influenced the whole world. However, by today's standards, certain parts of their preaching might in places come across as uncomfortable, questionable, or even downright offensive to some readers, the modern church being as broad and diverse in theological variety as it is.

I would firstly like to state that anything I have translated and paraphrased into the modern vernacular from Wesley's writings does not necessarily represent my views, but rather the views of the original writer, in the setting of their culture and place in history. I would secondly like to state that I have not reproduced these writings with any agenda, but rather for the sake of devotional study and academic curiosity concerning their doctrines and beliefs.

The sermons are translated sentence by sentence, carefully and prayerfully. The aim has been to communicate both word-for-word and thought-for-thought, choosing clarity of communication in simple English over archaic sentence structure where necessary, and preferring the original word order when there is no difference.

Wesley used the King James Bible in his original sermons, whereas to remain consistent with the word-for-word and thought-for-thought method used in these translations, the New International Version and New Living Translation have been used instead. Gender inclusive language has also been favoured over the archaic use of the word 'he' to indicate 'everyone'. The word 'humanity' has also been favoured over the word 'mankind', as this latter word now carries with it gender implications which were not present in Wesley's time. The complete original sermon is also included. Each time scripture is directly quoted, it is italicised.

Each sermon will be translated and published in order, from 1 to 44, and when the series is completed, they will be published as one volume.

In the meantime, I hope you are blessed, encouraged and challenged by the message of John Wesley, the man who completely changed the nation in which he lived. I hope you are spurred on to a zealous faith as you read how radical he was, and look back on the incredible fruit which his approach to Christian living bore for the Kingdom of God.

In Christ,

James Hargreaves

The Almost Christian (In Today's English)

Sermon 2 of 44

Introduction

Preached at St. Mary's, Oxford, before the University, on July 25th, 1741.

'Agrippa said to Paul, "You almost persuade me to become a Christian."' (Acts 26:28)

1:1. Today there are many who only go as far as Agrippa: ever since Christianity has existed there have been many people of every age and nationality who were almost persuaded to be Christians. Yet, as it achieves nothing in the sight of God to only go that far, it is extremely important for us to consider, -

1. What does it mean to be 'Almost a Christian?'

and

2. What does it mean to be 'Fully Christian?'[1]

---

[1] And many there are who go thus far: ever since the Christian religion was in the world, there have been many in every age and nation who were almost persuaded to be Christians. But seeing it avails nothing before God to go only thus far, it highly imports us to consider,

First. What is implied in being almost,

Secondly. What in being altogether, a Christian.

What Does It Mean To Be 'Almost Christian'?

2:1. Now, if someone is almost a Christian, we can assume at the very least that they have the basic human decency common among non-Christians. No-one, I expect will disagree with me here, especially as I am not suggesting that they follow the teachings of any non-Christian moral philosophers, but more that they know the behaviour they expect from others, and many of them actually act that way too. The rules of basic human decency taught them that they should be fair, that they should not steal from others, take unfair advantage of the under-privileged (financial or otherwise), nor be corrupt in business whether dealing with the poor or the rich. They also taught them the importance of every person's human rights, and how important it is, if at all possible, to stay out of debt.[2]

---

[2] 1. Now, in the being almost a Christian is implied, First, heathen honesty. No one, I suppose, will make any question of this; especially, since by heathen honesty here, I mean, not that which is recommended in the writings of their philosophers only, but such as the common heathens

15

2:2. Those without God's Word also accepted that truth and justice were important, and could not be completely disregarded. Therefore they despised anyone who swore by God when they were telling a lie, and anyone who slandered his friends or falsely accused another. Indeed, they considered intentional liars to be just as bad; a disgrace to humanity and pests in society.[3]

2:3. There was also a basic love and assistance which those without God expected from each other. They knew that if someone could help another, they should do so, regardless of how that person might be different. And this was the case

---

expected one of another, and many of them actually practised. By the rules of this they were taught that they ought not to be unjust; not to take away their neighbour's goods, either by robbery or theft; not to oppress the poor, neither to use extortion toward any; not to cheat or overreach either the poor or rich, in whatsoever commerce they had with them; to defraud no man of his right; and, if it were possible, to owe no man anything.

[3]   2. Again: the common heathens allowed, that some regard was to be paid to truth, as well as to justice. And, accordingly, they not only held him in abomination who was forsworn, who called God to witness to a lie; but him also who was known to be a slanderer of his neighbour, who falsely accused any man. And indeed, little better did they esteem wilful liars of any sort, accounting them the disgrace of human kind, and the pests of society.

both for the small, easy things which anyone can do for free, and for the much larger things. If they had food to spare, they knew it was right to share it with the hungry. If they had clothing to spare, they knew it was right to clothe those who had none. In general, they knew that if they had things which they did not need, it was right to give them to others in need. This is as far as the most simplistic non-Christian morality went. It only went as far as the very first step of being a Christian.[4]

2:4. The second thing which being 'Almost a Christian' implies, is having *a form of godliness* (2 Tim 3:5), that is, appearing on the outside to have a lifestyle which is very close to the teaching of Jesus in the gospels. The 'Almost

---

[4]   3. Yet again: there was a sort of love and assistance which they expected one from another. They expected whatever assistance any one could give another, without prejudice to himself. And this they extended not only to those little offices of humanity which are performed without any expense or labour, but likewise to the feeding the hungry, if they had food to spare; the clothing the naked with their own superfluous raiment; and, in general. the giving, to any that needed, such things as they needed not themselves. Thus far, in the lowest account of it, heathen honesty went; the first thing implied in the being almost a Christian.

Christians' therefore do nothing which Jesus taught against. They don't take God's Name in vain, they bless people and do not curse them, they do not swear by anyone or anything, but their 'yes' always means 'yes', and their 'no' always means 'no'. They don't do anything to break the Sabbath day of rest, nor do they allow anyone else in their household to, including their guests.[5]

Not only do they avoid any kind of sex outside of marriage, or sexual sin, but they avoid every word or glance which might directly or indirectly lead them to those things. They avoid all gossip, they don't belittle, backstab, spread rumours, or speak wickedly, and they avoid foolish talking and joking. Aristotle called this 'Eutrapelia', which briefly defined means steering

---

[5]   4. A second thing implied in the being almost a Christian, is, the having a form of godliness; of that godliness which is prescribed in the gospel of Christ; the having the outside of a real Christian. Accordingly, the almost Christian does nothing which the gospel forbids. he taketh not the name of God in vain; he blesseth, and curseth not; he sweareth not at all, but his communication is, yea, yea; nay, nay. he profanes not the day of the Lord, nor suffers it to be profaned, even by the stranger that is within his gates.

clear of all conversation that does not edify and therefore

'grieves the Holy Spirit of God, with whom we are sealed for

the day of redemption' (Eph 4:30).[6]

2:5. They refrain from drinking excessive amounts of alcohol, wild partying, and being greedy eaters. They avoid lying, fighting and arguing as much as they can manage, continually trying to live peacefully with everyone, and if someone wrongs them, they don't take revenge or try to 'even the score'. They are not verbally abusive, physically abusive, nor do they mock or gloat over anyone else's failings or misfortune. They do not intentionally cheat, hurt or distress anyone, but live in every way by that simple rule: *'Do to others as you would have them do to you'* (Lk 6:31).[7]

---

[6]   he not only avoids all actual adultery, fornication, and uncleanness, but every word or look that either directly or indirectly tends thereto; nay, and all idle words, abstaining both from detraction, backbiting, talebearing, evil speaking, and from "all foolish talking and jesting"--eutrapelia, a kind of virtue in the heathen moralist's account; -- briefly, from all conversation that is not "good to the use of edifying,' and that, consequently, "grieves the Holy Spirit of God, whereby we are sealed to the day of redemption.'

[7]   5. He abstains from "wine wherein is excess'; from revellings

2:6. In doing good, they don't only take the cheap and easy opportunities to show kindness, but they work and suffer so that many others might be blessed, and so that by their every effort someone may be helped. Whether it is difficult or painful, *'whatever their hand finds to do, they do with all their might'* (Ecc 9:10); whether for friends or enemies, for evil people or for good.[8]

Because they are not lazy in this or in anything they do, they take every opportunity to do every kind of good to every kind of person, and to their own souls and bodies. They sharply criticise those who are wicked, they teach the uneducated,

---

and gluttony. he avoids, as much as in him lies, all strife and contention, continually endeavouring to live peaceably with all men. And, if he suffer wrong, he avengeth not himself, neither returns evil for evil. he is no railer, no brawler, no scoffer, either at the faults or infirmities of his neighbour. he does not willingly wrong, hurt, or grieve any man; but in all things act and speaks by that plain rule, "Whatsoever thou wouldest not he should do unto thee, that do not thou to another."

[8]   6. And in doing good, he does not confine himself to cheap and easy offices of kindness, but labours and suffers for the profit of many, that by all means hae may help some. In spite of toil or pain, "whatsoever his hand findeth to do, he doeth it with his might;" whether it be for his friends, or for his enemies; for the evil, or for the good.

convince the undecided, encourage the good and comfort those who are suffering.[9]

They work to wake up the sleeping, and to lead those whom God has already woken to the *'Fountain opened to cleanse them from sin and impurity'* (Zech 13:1), where they can wash and be made clean. They also stimulate those who are saved by faith to glorify Christ and the gospel in everything they do.[10]

2:7. The person who has an outwardly Godly life also uses all of the 'Means of Grace' at every opportunity. They constantly attend church, but not as some people do: coming into the presence of the Most High weighed down with gold jewellery and expensive clothes, or in tasteless, flashy outfits. Either by

---

[9] For being "not slothful" in this, or in any "business," as he "hath opportunity" he doeth "good," all manner of good, "to all men;" and to their souls as well as their bodies. he reproves the wicked, instructs the ignorant, confirms the wavering, quickens the good, and comforts the afflicted.

[10] he labours to awaken those that sleep; to lead those whom God hath already awakened to the "Fountain opened for sin and for uncleanness," that they may wash therein and be clean; and to stir up those who are saved through faith, to adorn the gospel of Christ in all things.

being rude and antisocial or disrespectfully loud and silly they make no effort to have either the form of godliness or the power of godliness.[11]

I wish to God that there were no people here, even in this congregation who behaved that way! People who come into this church, and pay no attention to the service, staring off into space, restless with boredom (although occasionally they might offer a prayer asking God to bless something that they are about to do); people who, during that terribly boring service are either taking a nap, or laid back in their seats in the best possible position for one.[12]

---

[11]   7. He that hath the form of godliness uses also the means of grace; yea, all of them, and at all opportunities. he constantly frequents the house of God; and that, not as the manner of some is, who come into the presence of the Most High, either loaded with gold and costly apparel, or in all the gaudy vanity of dress, and either by their unseasonable civilities to each other, or the impertinent gaiety of their behaviour, disclaim all pretensions to the form as well as to the power of godliness.

[12]   Would to God there were none even among ourselves who fall under the same condemnation! who come into this house, it may be, gazing about, or with all the signs of the most listless, careless indifference, though sometimes they may seem to use a prayer to God for his blessing on what they are entering upon; who, during that awful service, are either asleep, or reclined in the most convenient posture for it;

They seem to think God is asleep. They openly have conversations during the meeting, or gaze aimlessly at the walls, totally vacant and uninterested. These people also don't have even the form of godliness. No, someone who has the form of godliness behaves seriously in that sacred service, and pays attention to the whole thing, especially when coming to take Holy Communion. This should never be taken lightly or carelessly, but with the attitude, posture and expression that only says, 'God, have mercy on me, a sinner!'[13]

2:8. If, along with this, someone has regular family prayer times, led by those who are in charge of their household, regular times of private prayer alone with God, and serious

---

[13] or, as though they supposed God was asleep, talking with one another, or looking round, as utterly void of employment. Neither let these be accused of the form of godliness. No; he who has even this, behaves with seriousness and attention, in every part of that solemn service. More especially, when he approaches the table of the Lord, it is not with a light or careless behaviour, but with an air, gesture, and deportment which speaks nothing else but "God be merciful to me a sinner!"

behaviour every day, they have the 'form of godliness' as long as they are consistent in it.[14]

---

[14]   8. To this, if we add the constant use of family prayer, by those who are masters of families, and the setting times apart for private addresses to God, with a daily seriousness of behaviour; he who uniformly practises this outward religion, has the form of godliness.

What Does It Mean To Be Fully Christian?

3:1. There is one thing more which will move someone from being 'Almost Christian' to being a full believer, and that is sincerity. By sincerity, I mean a real, heartfelt love for Jesus as the motive for their godly lifestyle. Indeed, if we don't have this, we don't even have the basic integrity of non-Christians; no, not enough of it to answer the challenge of a non-Christian Epicurean poet. Even this poor fool, in the few moments of clarity he had was able to observe:

'Good people avoid sin because they love goodness,

Wicked people avoid sin because they fear punishment.'[15]

---

[15]   There needs but one thing more in order to his being almost a Christian, and that is, sincerity. 9. By sincerity I mean, a real, inward principle of religion, from whence these outward actions flow. And, indeed if we have not this, we have not heathen honesty; no, not so much of it as will answer the demand of a heathen Epicurean poet. Even this poor wretch, in his sober intervals, is able to testify,
Oderunt peccare boni, virtutis amore;
Oderunt peccare mali, formidine poenae.

Therefore he concluded, if someone only holds back from doing evil to avoid the inevitable punishment, then not being punished is their reward. But even he does not consider such a man to be a good man, even by his non-Christian standards. So then, if someone not only commits no evil, but also does many good things, and uses all the 'Means of Grace', but does it all to avoid punishment, to avoid losing their friends, money, or reputation; then we could not truly say they are even an 'Almost a Christian!' If this is their only motivation for their lifestyle, they are nothing but a total hypocrite.[16]

3:2. If doing all these things without sincerity doesn't even make someone an 'Almost Christian', then sincerity is

---

[16]   So that, if a man only abstains from doing evil in order to avoid punishment, Non pasces in cruce corvos, [Thou shalt not be hanged.], saith the Pagan; there, "thou hast thy reward." But even he will not allow such a harmless man as this to be so much as a good heathen. If, then, any man, from the same motive, viz., to avoid punishment, to avoid the loss of his friends, or his gain, or his reputation, should not only abstain from doing evil, but also do ever so much good; yea, and use all the means of grace; yet we could not with any propriety say, this man is even almost a Christian. If he has no better principle in his heart, he is only a hypocrite altogether.

obviously essential to being 'Almost a Christian'; a serious

determination to serve God, a profound desire to do His will.

It is obviously necessary that someone desires wholeheartedly

to please Him in everything; in all their conversations,

actions, and in all that they do or leave undone. This goal

must be central to their entire lives, if they are to be Almost

Christians. This must be their motivation for doing good and

avoiding evil, and for obeying all the commands of God.[17]

3:3. At this point, some of you are probably thinking, 'How

could anyone possibly have such a radical lifestyle, and still

only be Almost a Christian?' What else could there

conceivably be to being a complete Christian? I answer that it

is indeed possible to be such a person, and still only be almost

---

[17]   10. Sincerity, therefore, is necessarily implied in the being
almost a Christian; a real design to serve God, a hearty desire to do his
will. It is necessarily implied, that a man have a sincere view of pleasing
God in all things; in all his conversation; in all his actions; in all he does or
leaves undone. This design, if any man be almost a Christian, runs through
the whole tenor of his life. This is the moving principle, both in his doing
good, his abstaining from evil, and his using the ordinances of God.

a Christian. I discovered this to be true not only in the words of the Bible, but also from my own personal experience.[18]

3:4. Brothers and sisters, I know I am taking a risk making such bold statements to you. However, please forgive me as I tell my own embarrassing story for the whole world to hear, for your sake and for the sake of the gospel. Please be patient with me as I talk openly about myself as if was someone else. I am content to look ridiculous so that you might be enlightened, and to be even more undignified for the glory of my Lord.[19]

---

[18] 11. But here it will probably be inquired, "Is it possible that any man living should go so far as this, and, nevertheless, be only almost a Christian What more than this, can be implied in the being a Christian altogether I answer, First, that it is possible to go thus far, and yet be but almost a Christian, I learn, not only from the oracles of God, but also from the sure testimony of experience.

[19] 12. Brethren, great is "my boldness towards you in this behalf." And "forgive me this wrong," if I declare my own folly upon the housetop, for yours and the gospel's sake. --Suffer me, then, to speak freely of myself, even as of another man. I am content to be abased, so ye may be exalted, and to be yet more vile for the glory of my Lord.

3:5. I did all these things I have described for many years, as many people here will be able to remember. I very carefully avoided all evil, keeping my conscience clean from causing offense, and making the most of all the time I had. I took advantage of every opportunity to do good to anyone and everyone, and meticulously used all the means of grace both private and public. I tried hard to be a man of serious behaviour in every time and place, and with God as my witness before whom I will one day stand, I did all these things with sincerity. I had a real desire to serve God, my heart was in it, I wanted to do His will in every part of my life and to please Him who called me to *'fight the good fight of the faith'* and to *'take hold of eternal life'* (1 Tim 6:12). Yet my own conscience was a witness against me, along with the Holy Spirit, that all that time I was still only Almost a Christian.[20]

---

[20]   13. I did go thus far for many years, as many of this place can testify; using diligence to eschew all evil, and to have a conscience void of offence; redeeming the time; buying up every opportunity of doing all good to all men; constantly and carefully using all the public and all the

3:6. If you want to know what more I needed to be completely Christian, I answer: Firstly, love for God. His word says, *'Love the Lord your God with all your heart and with all your soul and with all your strength and with all your mind'* (Lk 10:27). This kind of love preoccupies a person's whole heart, takes all their affection, fills every corner of their soul and uses their abilities to the absolute limit. If anyone loves the Lord their God in this way, their spirit will be constantly full of joy from God, their Saviour. They will be delighted by the Lord, their Master and their everything, to whom they are grateful, no matter what happens. All they want is God, and for others to know about Him.[21]

---

private means of grace; endeavouring after a steady seriousness of behaviour, at all times, and in all places; and, God is my record, before whom I stand, doing all this in sincerity; having a real design to serve God; a hearty desire to do his will in all things; to please him who had called me to "fight the good fight," and to "lay hold of eternal life." Yet my own conscience beareth me witness in the Holy Ghost, that all this time I was but almost a Christian.

[21]   1. If it be inquired, "What more than this is implied in the being altogether a Christian" I answer, First. The love of God. For thus saith his word, "Thou shalt love the Lord thy God with all thy heart, and with all thy soul, and with all thy mind, and with all thy strength." Such a love is this, as engrosses the whole heart, as rakes up all the affections, as fills the entire capacity of the soul and employs the utmost extent of all its

Their hearts are constantly crying out, *'Whom have I in heaven but you? And earth has nothing I desire besides you'* (Ps 73:25). Indeed, what can they desire other than God? Not the world, nor anything in the world, because they are crucified to the world, and the world is crucified to them (Gal 6:14). They are crucified to the *'craving for physical pleasure, the craving for everything they see, and pride in their achievements and possessions'* (1 John 2:16). Yes, they are dead to every kind of pride, because *'love is not proud'* (1 Cor 13:4); but someone who is in love with God, lives in God, and has God living in them too is worth less than nothing in their own eyes.[22]

---

faculties. he that thus loves the Lord his God, his spirit continually "rejoiceth in God his Saviour." his delight is in the Lord, his Lord and his All, to whom "in everything he giveth thanks. All his desire is unto God, and to the remembrance of his name."

[22]   his heart is ever crying out, "Whom have I in heaven but Thee and there is none upon earth that I desire beside Thee." Indeed, what can he desire beside God Not the world, or the things of the world: for he is "crucified to the world, and the world crucified to him." he is crucified to "the desire of the flesh, the desire of the eye, and the pride of life." Yea, he is dead to pride of every kind: for "love is not puffed up" but "he that dwelling in love, dwelleth in God, and God in him," is less than nothing in his own eyes.

3:7. The second thing required to be a complete Christian is love for one's neighbour. Jesus himself said it, using the following words, *'You shall love your neighbour as yourself.'* If anyone asks 'Who is my neighbour?', we reply, 'Every person in the world, every child of God, who is the Father of everyone's spirit.' We cannot exclude our enemies from this in any way, nor can we exclude God's enemies, or those who are enemies of their own souls, but instead every Christian should love those people as they love their own selves, yes, even as much as Christ loved them.[23]

If anyone wants to get a better grasp of the kind of love this is, they should read Paul the Apostle's description of it from 1 Corinthians 13. Love is *'patient and kind'*, it *'is not jealous'*,

---

[23]   2. The Second thing implied in the being altogether a Christian is, the love of our neighbour. For thus said our Lord in the following words, "Thou shalt love thy neighbour as thyself" If any man ask, "Who is my neighbour" we reply, Every man in the world; every child of his who is the Father of the spirits of all flesh. Nor may we in any wise except our enemies or the enemies of God and their own souls. But every Christian loveth these also as himself, yea, "as Christ loved us."

nor is it rash or quick to pass judgement on others. It 'is not proud', but makes whoever possesses it into the lowest rank: they become the servant of everyone. Love does not act in an inappropriate way, but becomes *all things to all men* (1 Cor 9:22). Love does not insist on it's own way, but only seeks the good of others, so that they will be saved. Love does not get provoked. Those without enough love experience rage, but love drives rage away. Love does not think evil things, it does not take pleasure in sin, but finds joy in the truth. *It always protects, always trusts, always hopes, always perseveres.* [24]

3:8. There is however, one more thing which we can look at separately (although it can't actually be separated from what

---

[24]   he that would more fully understand what manner of love this is, may consider St. Paul's description of it. It is "long-suffering and kind." It "envieth not." It is not rash or hasty in judging. It "is not puffed up;" but maketh him that loves, the least, the servant of all. Love "doth not behave itself unseemly," but becometh "all things to all men." She "seeketh not her own;" but only the good of others, that they may be saved. "Love is not provoked." It casteth out wrath, which he who hath is wanting in love. "It thinketh no evil. It rejoiceth not in iniquity, but rejoiceth in the truth. It covereth all things, believeth all things, hopeth all things, endureth all things."

we have already discussed), which is essential to being a complete Christian. It is the very foundation of everything; it is faith.[25]

The Bible says incredible things about faith. John the beloved disciple wrote; *'Everyone who believes that Jesus is the Christ is born of God'* (1 John 5:1), *'to all who received him, to those who believed in his name, he gave the right to become children of God'* (1 John 1:12), and *'this is the victory that has overcome the world, even our faith'* (1 John 5:4). Yes, the Lord Himself said, *'I tell you the truth, whoever hears my word and believes him who sent me has eternal life and will not be condemned; he has crossed over from death to life'* (John 5:24).[26]

---

[25]   3. There is yet one thing more that may be separately considered, though it cannot actually be separate from the preceding, which is implied in the being altogether a Christian; and that is the ground of all, even faith.

[26]   Very excellent things are spoken of this throughout the oracles of God. "Every one, saith the beloved disciple, "that believeth is born of God." "To as many as received him, gave he power to become the sons of God. even to them that believe on his name." And "this is the victory that overcometh the world, even our faith." Yea, our Lord himself declares, "He that believeth in the Son hath everlasting life; and cometh not into

3:9. But don't deceive yourselves about this, we must be careful to remember that a faith which does not bring about repentance, love, and every kind of good work is not the real, living faith, but is a dead, demonic one. For even the demons believe in the virgin birth of Christ, and that He performed all kinds of miracles, proving Himself to be God, and that He did it for our sakes. They believe that He endured an incredibly painful death to save us from everlasting destruction, that He rose again on the third day, that He rose to heaven where He is seated on the right side of the Father, and that at the end of the world He will return again to judge the living and the dead. These parts of our faith the demons believe too, and they also believe everything written in the Old and New Testaments, yet even knowing all these things they remain demons. They remain in their doomed state, lacking the real and true Christian faith.[27]

---

condemnation, but is passed from death unto life."
[27]   4. But here let no man deceive his own soul. "It is diligently to be noted, the faith which bringeth not forth repentance, and love, and all good works, is not that right living faith, but a dead and devilish one. For,

3:10. To quote the words of the Anglican Church, 'The correct and real Christian faith is not only to believe that the Bible and the Articles of Faith are true, but also to be convinced and confident that you have been saved from eternity in Hell by Christ.' We can be certain and confident that by the goodness of Christ, God has forgiven our sins, and returned us to a place of favour with Him; and from that place flows the loving desire to follow His commandments.[28]

3:11. So, who is not an Almost Christian, but a true Christian? Whoever has this faith which, by the power of God living

---

even the devils believe that Christ was born of a virgin: that he wrought all kinds of miracles, declaring himself very God: that, for our sakes, he suffered a most painful death, to redeem us from death everlasting; that he rose again the third day: that he ascended into heaven, and sitteth at the right hand of the Father and at the end of the world shall come again to judge both the quick and dead. These articles of our faith the devils believe, and so they believe all that is written in the Old and New Testament. And yet for all this faith, they be but devils. They remain still in their damnable estate lacking the very true Christian faith."

[28]   5. "The right and true Christian faith is (to go on m the words of our own Church), "not only to believe that Holy Scripture and the Articles of our Faith are true, but also to have a sure trust and confidence to be saved from everlasting damnation by Christ. It is a sure trust and confidence which a man hath in God, that, by the merits of Christ, his sins are forgiven, and he reconciled to the favour of God; whereof doth follow a loving heart, to obey his commandments."

within them cleanses their hearts from pride, rage, lust, from everything which is not righteous, and from all things physically and spiritually unclean. Whoever has a heart filled with love stronger than death for both God and humanity; love that does the same things God does and is happy to exhaust all it has for the sake of others. Whoever joyfully endures being mocked, held in contempt and hated by everyone because they belong to Christ, and embraces whatever suffering God, in His wisdom, allows people and demons to inflict upon them. Whoever has a faith that does all these things, with love as their motive, is not Almost, but truly Christian.[29]

---

[29]   6. Now, whosoever has this faith, which "purifies the heart" (by the power of God, who dwelleth therein) from "pride, anger, desire, from all unrighteousness" from "all filthiness of flesh and spirit;" which fills it with love stronger than death, both to God and to all mankind; love that doeth the works of God, glorying to spend and to be spent for all men, and that endureth with joy, not only the reproach of Christ, the being mocked, despised, and hated of all men, but whatsoever the wisdom of God permits the malice of men or devils to inflict, --whosoever has this faith thus working by love is not almost only, but altogether, a Christian.

In Closing

4:1. But who alive can say they know anyone who does all these things? I beg you, brothers and sisters, remembering *'Even Death and Destruction hold no secrets from the LORD. How much more does he know the human heart!'* (Prov 15:11), ask yourselves in the deepest place, 'Am I an Almost Christian?' Do I even keep the basic non-Christian rules about being fair, compassionate and honest? If so, do I act like a Christian on the outside? Do I have the 'form of godliness'? Do I avoid all evil, and whatever is forbidden in the Bible? Do I take every opportunity to do good with all my passion and energy? Do I take advantage of every chance to obey the commands of God? And if so, do I act from the sincere motive and desire to please God in everything?[30]

---

[30]   7. But who are the living witnesses of these things I beseech you, brethren, as in the presence of that God before whom "hell and destruction are without a covering--how much more the hearts of the children of men" --that each of you would ask his own heart, "Am I of that number Do I so far practise justice, mercy, and truth, as even the rules of heathen honesty require If so, have I the very outside of a Christian the form of godliness

4:2. Right now, aren't many of you realising that you have never even been this far; that you have never even been an 'Almost Christian'? That you have not even lived to the standard of non-Christian integrity, or at least, you have not lived up to the standard of having the form of Christian godliness? God has hardly ever seen sincerity in you; a real deep desire to please Him in everything. You never intended to use all of your words, actions, work, studies and times of recreation for His glory. You never planned or wished to do everything *in the name of the Lord Jesus'*, nor did you desire that your life should be *'a spiritual sacrifice, acceptable to God through Jesus Christ'* (1 Pet 2:5).[31]

Do I abstain from evil, --from whatsoever is forbidden in the written Word of God Do I, whatever good my hand findeth to do, do it with my might Do I seriously use all the ordinances of God at all opportunities And is all this done with a sincere design and desire to please God in all things"
[31]   8. Are not many of you conscious, that you never came thus far; that you have not been even almost a Christian; that you have not come up to the standard of heathen honesty; at least, not to the form of Christian godliness --much less hath God seen sincerity in you, a real design of pleasing him in all things. You never so much as intended to devote all your words and works. your business, studies, diversions, to his glory. You never even designed or desired, that whatsoever you did should be done "in the name of the Lord Jesus, and as such should be "a spiritual sacrifice, acceptable to God through Christ.

4:3. But let's assume for a minute that you did plan and desire these things, do those desires alone make you a Christian? In no way whatsoever, unless they are acted upon. Someone once said, 'The road to Hell is paved with good intentions.'[32] The greatest question of all of them however, is 'does love for God fill your heart?' Can you cry out, 'My God and my Everything'? Do you want nothing other than Him? Are you satisfied with God? Is He your pride, your delight, the crowning joy of your life? And is this command also in your heart; *'Whoever loves God must also love their Christian brothers and sisters'?* (1 John 4:21)[33]

Do you therefore love your neighbour as yourself? Do you love everyone, including your enemies and God's enemies, as much as you love your own soul? As much as Christ loved

---

[32]   9. But, supposing you had, do good designs and good desires make a Christian By no means, unless they are brought to good effect. "Hell is paved," saith one, "with good intentions."

[33]   The great question of all, then, still remains. Is the love of God shed abroad in your heart Can you cry out, "My God, and my All" Do you desire nothing but him Are you happy in God Is he your glory, your delight, your crown of rejoicing And is this commandment written in your heart, "That he who loveth God love his brother also"

you? Indeed, do you believe that Jesus loved you, and gave Himself for you? Do you believe in His blood? Do you believe that the Lamb of God has taken away your sins, and buried them like a stone dropped into the deepest ocean? Do you believe that he has wiped away the charges against you, taking them from your future and nailing them to His cross? Have you truly been ransomed from Hell by His blood, which was shed for your sins? And does the Holy Spirit confirm to your spirit that you are a child of God?[34]

4:4. The God and Father of our Lord Jesus Christ, who is now standing among us, knows that if anyone dies without this kind of faith and love, it would have been better for that

---

[34] Do you then love your neighbour as yourself Do you love every man, even your enemies, even the enemies of God, as your own soul as Christ loved you Yea, dost thou believe that Christ loved thee, and gave himself for thee Hast thou faith in his blood Believest thou the Lamb of God hath taken away thy sins, and cast them as a stone into the depth of the sea that he hath blotted out the handwriting that was against thee, taking it out of the way, nailing it to his cross Hast thou indeed redemption through his blood, even the remission of thy sins And doth his Spirit bear witness with thy spirit, that thou art a child of God

person to have never been born. Wake up then, you who are sleeping, and cry out to God: cry out to Him while He can still be found. Give Him no rest until like Moses, He makes all of His goodness appear before you, until He tells you His name: *'The Lord, the Lord, the compassionate and gracious God, slow to anger, abounding in love and faithfulness, maintaining love to thousands, and forgiving wickedness, rebellion and sin'* (Ex 34:6-7).[35]

Let no-one discourage you with false words to settle for anything less than the complete fulfilment of your high calling. Instead, cry out to Him both day and night until you know the One you believe in, and can say 'My Lord and my God!' Always remember to pray and not to give up, until you

---

[35] 10. The God and Father of our Lord Jesus Christ, who now standeth in the midst of us, knoweth, that if any man die without this faith and this love, good it were for him that he had never been born. Awake, then, thou that sleepest, and call upon thy God: call in the day when he may be found. Let him not rest, till he make his "goodness to pass before thee;" till he proclaim unto thee the name of the Lord, "The Lord, the Lord God, merciful and gracious, long-suffering, and abundant in goodness and truth, keeping mercy for thousands, forgiving iniquity, and transgression, and sin."

can raise your hands to the skies and say to Him who lives

forever and ever, *'Lord, you know all things, you know that I*

love you' (John 21:17).[36]

4:5. May we experience what it is to be a true Christian, not

merely an 'Almost Christian.' May we be filled with joy at

the thought of one day seeing God in His glory, for we have

been made right with Him freely because of His undeserved

favour. May we know that we have peace with God because

of the reconciliation that came through Jesus Christ, and may

the love of God fill our hearts, through the Holy Spirit who

has been given to us![37]

---

[36]   Let no man persuade thee, by vain words, to rest short of this prize of thy high calling. But cry unto him day and night, who, "while we were without strength, died for the ungodly," until thou knowest in whom thou hast believed, and canst say, "My Lord, and my God!" Remember, "always to pray, and not to faint," till thou also canst lift up thy hand unto heaven, and declare to him that liveth for ever and ever, "Lord, Thou knowest all things, Thou knowest that I love Thee."

[37]   11. May we all thus experience what it is to be, not almost only; but altogether Christians; being justified freely by his grace, through the redemption that is in Jesus; knowing we have peace with God through Jesus Christ; rejoicing in hope of the glory of God; and having the love of God shed abroad in our hearts, by the Holy Ghost given unto us!

9421083R00027

Printed in Great Britain
by Amazon.co.uk, Ltd.,
Marston Gate.